OVERSIZE

712

D0316595

THE BOOK OF
GARDENS
A photographic collection

by Siobhan Buchanan-Johnston
words by Tracy Biggam

MPG

MONTAGUE
PUBLICATIONS
GROUP

"Show me your garden and I shall tell you what you are."

Alfred Austin

The poet Alfred Austin was struck by the intimacy of the relationship between a garden and the gardener and what the former could reveal about the latter. Sadly my own garden reveals that I have too little time to devote to tending its every need, but what it doesn't say about me is how much I love looking at a beautiful garden. I wanted this book to appeal as much to people like me, who garden only in their heads, as to those who regularly feel the soil in their hands. I am not a gardener and nor can I profess to any amount of horticultural knowledge, but I know what my ultimate garden looks like. In The Book of Gardens I have tried to include a garden for everyone, from the tiniest space in the city to country gardens rambling over several acres. Rather than instruction, this book is about inspiration; it's about looking at a beautiful garden and imagining it was yours. There's no gardening advice here, nor hundreds of Latin plant names, as I my vision was to produce a piece of beautiful escapism: a book to reside on the coffee table and be returned to again and again.

Siobhan Buchanan-Johnston

Thank you,

To Tracy Biggam for her time, wonderful words and inspiration and her great company and laughs on our many trips!. To Sean Briethaupt and Yvette Monaghan from Studio Seventy Seven Photography for their huge commitment, beautiful pictures and their hours and hours of devotion (rain, hail or shine) to capturing that perfect garden shot. To photographer Helen Fickling also for her huge and valued contribution. To Barry Murphy for, of course, great photography and best technical support!! To everyone involved from Montague Publications Group,- Richard Harris, Grainne Clarke, Fiona Masterson and a very special thank you to designer Michal Swoboda.

Also thanks to The Chelsea Flower Show and The Royal Horticultural Society, The Bloom Garden Festival, Bord Bia, The Royal Horticultural Society Ireland, Stena Line and The Rockwell Hotel, London.

publishing director
siobhan buchanan-johnston
director
david sinclair
editor
siobhan buchanan-johnston
features editor
tracy biggam
group commercial manager
richard harris
design
michal swoboda
distribution and marketing
gráinne clarke
fiona masterson

The Book Of Gardens is published by
Montague Publications Group,
39 Fitzwilliam Street Upper, Dublin 2, Ireland.
tel: +353 1 669 2101 fax: +353 1 669 2104
www.montaguegroup.ie

gardens in the urban landscape

gardens on show

gardens with a story to tell

gardens in the urban landscape

wall to wall

" *This is the garden: colours come and go,*

   frail azures fluttering from night's outer wing,

   strong silent greens serenely lingering,

   absolute lights like baths of golden snow..."

E.E. Cummings "This is the garden".

In her south London garden, photographer Helen Fickling has combined geometric design and bold use of colour with restrained planting, to produce a visually arresting garden which functions on many different levels.

Helen and designer, Catherine Heatherington, who helped create the geometric pattern and structure of the garden, are both admirers of the work of the Mexican architect, Luis Barragan, and it is easy to see how his style has been instrumental in inspiring the almost installation-like feel of this small city garden.

With a space measuring 6m wide and 25m long, a key objective of the design was to create as much visual width as possible. To this end a daring architectural feature in the form of a giant crimson wall, is set at an angle, mid-way down the garden, almost bisecting the space and tempting the eye to try and glimpse what lies beyond. Elongated windows cut into the wall lighten its structure and permit narrow vistas from one end of the garden to the other.

Another wall, this time in glowing, mild rusted steel, designed and built by art metal worker, Louis Calmels, creates an angle from the opposite side. The two walls almost form a t-shape and are prevented from touching by a narrow pathway of Balau hardwood which leads to the black-lined, trapezium-shaped pool running across the width of the garden.

Water gushes from a steel spout fixed high up on the tall dark wall at the head of the pool. Unseen from the house, the soothing sound of cascading water draws the visitor down to the broad, sun-bathed Balau wood deck at the end of the garden. Planting is dominated by clipped box hedging which complements the geometric design, providing year-round colour and a natural foil for the strong colours of the hard landscaping. Close to the house and enclosing a paved terrace abutting the conservatory kitchen, the buxus has been laid out in a grid of square metre blocks, clustering in occasional domed shapes.

More box flanks the boardwalk leading to the pool with beds on either side. Against the shadier wall stand three tree ferns, underplanted with a variety of other ferns and Euphorbia robii. A plantswoman at heart, Helen has reserved the bed on the opposing side, south of the crimson wall, as a place in the garden to experiment with different planting combinations. In late summer the bed has an almost wild feel to it, with a vivid tangle of bronze fennel and Verbena bonariensis sprouting up amongst grasses and night-scented tobacco plants.

moonstruck

" A full-orbed moon, that like thine own soul soaring,

Sought a precipitate pathway up through heaven,

There fell a silvery silken veil of light,

With quietude, and sultriness and slumber,

Upon the upturn'd faces of a thousand

Roses that grew in an enchanted garden..."

Edgar Allen Poe: "A Moon Poem".

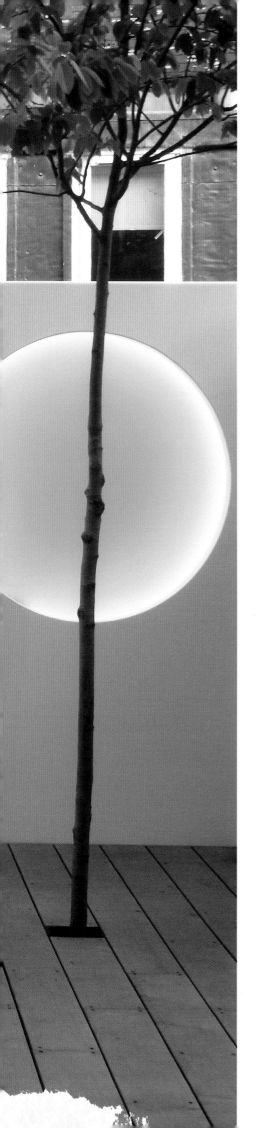

What the city garden may lack in terms of size of space, it often gains in a more imaginative use of the space that exists. At this first floor garden in north London, designer Andy Sturgeon has created a suspended outdoor room, complete with omnipresent glowing 'moon', which gives his clients a private place to eat and entertain outdoors, surrounded by the roof tops of the city. Down a narrow laneway in an affluent part of town where tall houses stand cheek by jowl, opportunities for garden creation are somewhat limited and maximising even the most obscure space is crucial to provide a spot in which to enjoy a fine summer's evening.

At 4m x 4m, this garden is really only a generously sized balcony, but Sturgeon's uncluttered, contemporary design has created a dynamic outdoor space where plants grow happily in irrigated flower beds rather than pots and a barbecue can be enjoyed in the shade of a leafy tree.

Different wall treatments are the key to giving depth to the space – louvered trellises allow in wind and light to create a feeling of openness and a white powder-coated metal panel encloses an acrylic sheet containing a circular neon light, to provide sculptural interest day and night.

The clients were keen to keep the design as minimalist as possible, with low levels of mainly green planting. To this end there are simply shallow beds of bamboo and herbs which are sunk into cedar decking and a single Amelanchier, or snowy mespilus tree, which obligingly produces white flowers in spring and early summer and colourful leaves and berries in the autumn.

a seamless blend

"*And now to sum up as to a garden…*
It should by no means imitate either
the wilfulness or the wildness of Nature,
but should look like a thing never to be
seen except near a house. It should,
in fact, look like a part of the house."

William Morris "Hopes and Fears for Art" 1882.

A tiny courtyard garden, 300m from the sea at Brighton, has been transformed into an outdoor breakfast room and entertainment space by its owner, garden designer, Patrick Clarke.

With the courtyard measuring a mere 5m x 5m, the focus of Clarke's design was to visually enlarge the space by pushing any ornamentation, be it in the form of planting or hard landscaping, to the perimeters, leaving the centre free. Also fundamental to the scheme was a requirement for the garden to be linked visually to the house in a seamless continuation of the interior. In line with these twin objectives, a copper covered work bench appears to extend outwards from the kitchen, running along one side wall of the garden at the same height and depth as the kitchen work surface. Iroko panelled cupboards beneath the bench are designed to hide all-manner of objects to keep the garden clutter-free, from a bicycle to a dog kennel, and more iroko is used above the bench to provide screening. The key aesthetics of the design are a central black slate terrace, flanked by pebble-mulched beds, each planted in shades of green with a variety of ferns on one side and a spiky row of Miscanthus sinensis 'Zebrinus' on the other. To complement the style of the garden is a table and stool set, designed by Clarke, which has been custom-made from strips of light birch ply resting on slender steel frames.

a city haven

" *Surrender yourself to stillness, the truth you seek is already there...* "

An ancient Zen koan

Hidden away behind a row of Georgian buildings in a quiet corner of west London is the Hempel Hotel. Just a stone's throw away, in the tree-lined central enclave of the square, is the hotel's tranquil, Zen-inspired garden.

Designed by Anouska Hempel, this quintessential boutique hotel opened in 1996 and imbued the essence of pared down minimalism. Influenced by her travels to Japan, the designer infused a far eastern perfume throughout the hotel, both inside and out. The garden was conceived as a theatre for outdoor entertaining and is a harmonious fusion of minimalist and classical styles with Japanese detailing. Hempel and garden design consultants, Landuse, developed a design of restrained simplicity, wholly portrayed in green and white, using symmetry, form and texture to create impact.

Three square lawns, with dark, inky pools at the centre of each, appear jewel-like when viewed from above. Framed and edged with crushed white Portland Stone paths, immaculately raked as in the best traditions of Zen gardening, the trio of lawn squares is enclosed by clipped box hedging with trees behind, pruned to allow light to penetrate. Off-setting the geometric lines of the parterre, spheres of Portland Stone are carefully placed at intervals and the squat green curves of domed topiary sit all around, providing infinite texture as the sun's rays caress their rounded forms in a halo-like effect.

The hotel's building and garden are both remarkable pieces of engineering, united by a serenity which conceals the machinery of modern living. At the heart of the hotel a colossal Portland Stone-clad void soars in unbroken form ever upward and in the stillness of the garden, the visitor remains blissfully unaware that the District Line runs just beneath its calm symmetry.

" Even if you imitate nature perfectly, it isn't art –
you've got to have a little magic and go beyond
nature to create atmosphere."

Patrick Watson, landscape designer.

For one residence at a 1950s-styled development in the leafy, affluent Johannesburg suburb of Sandhurst, Patrick Watson has designed a spectacular 'fantasy' garden where wild nature meets film star glamour. Watson is South Africa's most celebrated landscape designer and acknowledged to be amongst the World's most influential. His work cannot be characterised by one particular genre, as something unique seems to emerge with each new project. A kaleidoscope of different styles, from formal English gardens to tropical jungles, Zen gardens and golf courses, all feature in an extraordinary portfolio developed over the past 30 years, during which time he has worked for world leaders, royal princes and billionaire developers. There is still always time in Watson's world, however, for the micro-climate of the private individual, as in his work at this suburban garden.

The client's twin passions - for Japan and the African bush - were key influences in the design, whereby a 300m^2 arid plot of red dust was transformed into a magical oasis. Watson's admiration for the work of the Californian modernist, Thomas Church, is well known, and the great man's influence is evident here at Sandton House, where Watson has abstracted the rugged landscape of his native South Africa, incorporating symbolic elements of rock and water within the garden, just as Church echoed the mountains of California in his design at the famous Donnell garden, 'El Novillero'.

Water is the focal element in the garden's design, and has been used by Watson to unify the thundering heartbeat of the African bush with the serene tranquillity of the Japanese Zen garden. His connection between the two is a symbolic Orange River (one of South Africa's most spectacular natural features) which greets you at the entrance and whose journey is re-created in miniature, linking the disparate elements of the garden through its meandering path. Fed by gurgling tributaries, a frothy stream rushes away from the bridge at the entrance. After passing ancient rocks of monolithic proportions, it disappears under the house before re-emerging in a luscious pastureland of Japanese tufted grass, populated by rare Crinum lilies. From there the water stampedes on, over giant sienna-hued boulders and through a granite gorge where gnarled trees grow out of dark crevices and moisture-loving plants cling precariously to mossy rock formations, before reaching journey's end at a silent pool, where golden Koi Carp glide under purple drifts of Jacaranda flowers in the shade of black bamboo.

A series of curving terraces links the garden to the house at different levels and one extravagant, sweeping timber deck fans out from the house to the edge of a cobalt blue, '50s-style infinity pool, its motionless surface glistening invitingly under the balcony of the first floor master bedroom. "This garden is like a goldfish bowl," Watson explains. "It was made for showing off ..."

structure and harmony

" I don't divide architecture, landscape and gardening; to me they are one."

Luis Barragan.

The name Christopher Bradley-Hole is synonymous with minimalist garden design. Indeed Patrick Taylor in "The Oxford Companion to the Garden", describes him as: "… the most significant proponent of minimalist gardens in late 20th and early 21st century Britain." Renowned for his use of the golden section to divide space and thus create harmony, Bradley-Hole designs gardens which are uncompromisingly minimalist yet full of texture, colour and detail and where planting is used to reinforce the design rather than being eschewed as unnecessary embellishment. His garden at an early Victorian villa in North London was designed to complement a contemporary ground floor extension to the building. The steel-framed extension, by Eric Parry Architects, was built to the full width of the site, adding a sequence of light-filled spaces for both entertaining and family life. Each window in the extension has full elevation frameless glass panes which enables a strong relationship to be established betweenthe house and the garden. Designed on three levels to produce a succession of clearly defined, yet complementary spaces which reflect their differing usage and varying relationships to the building, the garden is uncluttered and effortlessly free-flowing.

Sparing use of block colour and a restricted range of repeating materials combine to produce both impact and harmony. Upper and lower terraces in stone and timber adjoin the house (the upper being a roof terrace above the extension), with an elevated grassed terrace running the width of the site between the lower terrace and the boundary wall. At ground level, the garden has been designed to relate closely to the interiors of the house, dividing into two distinct areas - doors from the kitchen open out onto the warm tones of cedar boards while those from the art-filled drawing room on the same level meet the cool formality of Portuguese limestone. The simple elegance of a limestone bench further defines the two areas. Standing tall above the ground floor terrace, a pair of raised beds flanks a central limestone stairway containing two flights of steps, cut at different heights, to add architectural detail. The bed rising from the cedar decking has a specialist red Venetian plaster finish which is echoed in a feature "blade" wall against the rear boundary of the grassed level above, whilst the opposing bed flows upwards, as a continuation of the limestone terrace. Limestone steps at either side of the terrace enable the garden to be toured in a circuit and provide access to a spa and gym beneath, whilst reinforced glass panels allow light to filter below. Above, at first floor level, another timber and limestone terrace of Zen-like simplicity looks down over the garden. In a geometric arrangement, precision-cut stone benches and beds of taxus hedging define areas within the terrace, which is also inset with reinforced glass panels and rectilinear flat beds of smooth pebbles. A glass balustrade all the way around affords glimpses of Bradley-Hole's trademark naturalistic perennial planting in the beds below and delivers a clear view of the grassed terrace – the children's play area – with its orderly row of pleached hornbeams sitting in pebbled squares.

" *Every garden-maker should be an artist along his own lines. That is the only possible way to create a garden, irrespective of size or wealth.*"

Vita Sackville-West

Peter Kruseman would be the first to confess that he doesn't know the names of too many of the plants in his garden, but as a design consultant, he does understand concepts, shapes and colour and he has used these skills in the development of his coastal acre.

In 2003, when they moved into their newly-constructed house at Greystones, Co Wicklow, Peter and wife Nicky, an artist, found they had the gardening equivalent of a blank canvas to play with, as the builder's idea of landscaping had been merely to throw a scattering of earth over the site prior to departure. It was a site with a lot going for it, however, as although seaside gardens are often restricted in terms of planting possibilities, the Krusemans' garden, perched above Greystones' North Shore, is fortuitously situated to be relatively sheltered from the prevailing winds, yet blessed with an abundance of natural light and stunning views out to sea.

Approaching his garden as he would any other design project, Peter first toured the site, studying the aspect of each part. He took photographs as he went which he then enlarged to form a backdrop for his concepts and also cut out images from magazines which were used to develop mood boards. Finally, he wrote out a detailed brief for garden designer Philip Brightling and plants specialist, Brian Wood. The resulting garden is really not one, but five converging gardens, situated at the rear and sea-facing side of the house, which Peter labelled in his brief as the 'House Terrace Garden', the 'Exotic Garden', the 'Mediterranean Garden', the 'Irish Garden' and the 'Asian Garden' and then went on to describe how he intended to use each one, whether as a "me garden" (for quiet contemplation or as a "we garden" (for entertaining family and friends). A gravelled area at the front of the house, planted with clumps of sun-loving, drought-tolerant varieties, such as agapanthus, lavenders and the occasional agave, continues around to the side where a Mediterranean feel has been established with groups of terracotta pots and raised beds containing an orderly row of olive trees, under-planted with lavender. Closer in to the house a decked area with sunken contemplative pools sparsely planted with white iris is the focus for the Asian Garden with its eastern-inspired rattan furniture. Evening gatherings here are illuminated by the light cast from nearby brick fire-pits and elegant glass globe night lights.

The steeply sloping ground at the rear of the house has been cut to form three levels, accessed by centrally located stone steps which rise up from a long terrace, paved with Indian 'Mint' Sandstone. Above, are the Exotic and Irish gardens, distinguishable by the jungle-like appearance of the former, with its tangle of friendly giants like the honey bush, Melianthus major, and azaleas, fuschias and viburnums in the latter. Below, mixed herbaceous and shrub planting forms an explosion of colour, where bright pink persicarias compete for impact with the foaming lime green of Alchemilla mollis and tall waving grasses and pencil thin cypress trees vary the heights in-between.

Towering above all, is a decadent garden retreat in the shape of a wooden day-bed, its white cotton hangings fluttering in the breeze. Erected originally for a party, the bed has become an oft-frequented part of the landscape.

gardens on show

" *The Pedigree of Honey*

Does not concern the Bee —

A Clover, any time, to him,

Is Aristocracy ... "

Emily Dickinson "The Bee".

As part of the celebrations for their tercentenary, the world-famous department store, Fortnum & Mason, commissioned garden designer and landscape architect, Robert Myers, to design a garden for the Chelsea Flower Show 2007 that would reflect 'Fortnum's' in the twenty first century as well as harking back to its eighteenth century beginnings.

Amongst the most photographed ornamental garden features at Chelsea 2007 were the four eau de nil 'Fortnum & Mason beehives' in this garden, each fashioned in a different neo-classical style. They will eventually be put to work on the roof of 181 Piccadilly, but here the beehives are an important influence in both the garden's structural design and planting.

The garden is set out on a simple, axial plan and has a distinctly 'historical' elegance with a contemporary twist. A central grass path, flanked on both sides by colourful planting, leads up the middle of the garden to a paved terrace, which forms the focal viewpoint. A balustraded wall at the rear of the terrace has been planted with pleached, feathered Liquidambar trees and these are trained around three Georgian-inspired shell and pebble grotto niches. Where the beehives stand, the garden is bordered by an oak and wicker fence with a hedge of pleached lime trees standing in front. Gently curving pebble mosaic paths cross from side to side, creating different views and vistas as they lead to each beehive, simultaneously providing access for maintenance.

Planting in the main flower beds is designed to include nectar-rich varieties attractive to bees whilst creating a 'tapestry' of rich colours and textures, in a palette dominated by red, purple, pink and pale yellow. The plants are arranged in drifts, as preferred by bees and the arrangement is punctuated by the columnar shapes of five fastigiate hornbeams which act as vertical counterpoints to the horizontal waves of planting and also frame various views within the garden.

an english garden

" This place is a jungle of beauty ... I cannot hope to describe it in words, for indeed it is an impossible thing to reproduce the shape, colour, depth and design of such a garden through the poor medium of prose."

Vita Sackville-West, writing about Hidcote Manor Garden in 1948.

For many it is Hidcote Manor Garden that best represents the quintessential twentieth century English garden style. Buried deep in the Cotswolds, this Arts & Crafts garden is an unfolding floral paradise which has become a mecca for garden lovers the world over. Chris Beardshaw's garden at Chelsea 2007 – "Celebrating 100 years of Hidcote Manor" delivers a tantalising taste of Hidcote and reflects the centenary restoration programme which is returning the garden to the way it would have looked in creator Lawrence Johnston's time.

At Hidcote, Johnston had created the archetypal 'garden of rooms' - twenty eight of them, each with its own unique style. Following suit, Beardshaw's garden is divided into three distinctly different areas, linked via narrow doorways to hide and surprise in turn.

Echoing Hidcote's 'Pillar Garden', the first room is filled by a pair of intensely and exuberantly planted herbaceous borders in vibrant and clashing colours - oranges, lime greens and purples - set against a formal backdrop of dark taxus hedging. Next door, the scene is the tranquil 'Theatre Lawn' where a replica of one of Johnston's trademark red brick pavilions nestles between high hedges of pleached hornbeams with a rectangle of green lawn stretched out in front. The shady woodland garden is the last room to be reached with informal planting where rich colours give way to a palette of cool blues and yellows.

natural habitat

" *A garden saw I full of blosmy boughs*

Upon a river, in a grene mead,

There as sweetness evermore enow is,

With flowers white, blue, yellow, and red,

And colde welle-streames, nothing dead,

That swimmen full of smale fishes light,

With finnes red, and scales silver bright..."

Geoffrey Chaucer "Love's Garden".

In springtime, the wild flowers on Californian hillsides burst into a rich tapestry of colour, and it was this natural habitat, portrayed in the context of an eco-friendly vineyard, that designer Kate Frey wanted to recreate for her garden, 'The Fetzer Sustainable Winery Garden', at the Chelsea Flower Show 2007.

The garden's focal point is a rustic winery made from recycled redwood and around it three different ecological habitats have been created to symbolise a dry and infertile vineyard, a moist meadow and a wetland area. The result is an explosion of colour in a nostalgic rural setting as 83 wild species, such as Californian poppies, poached egg flowers and crimson clovers, all vie for attention.

a plantsman's garden

" If I'm ever reborn, I want to be a gardener –
there's too much to do for one lifetime!"

Karl Foerster

Karl Foerster's garden at his home in Potsdam-Bormim, Germany, was the inspiration for "The Daily Telegraph Garden" at Chelsea 2007. The design, by Gabriella Pape and Isabelle Van Groeningen, features a sunken garden with a formal geometric framework and aims to use Foerster's principles in creating a plantsman's garden that has one metaphorical foot in the British Isles and the other on German soil. Foerster was a plantsman 'par excellence' and is just as revered in northern Europe for his skill, as his contemporary, Gertrude Jekyll, is in the UK. But whilst Jekyll was a great colourist, Foerster selected his plants based first and foremost on how well he thought they would thrive in a particular situation. A summary, stereotyping the two methods, is that the English garden with their hearts and the Germans with their heads. What Pape and Van Groeningen aimed to show in this garden is that plant design can be guided by both heart and mind. Colour, shape and texture can be combined naturally with moisture, drought and shade to produce a garden pleasing to the eye … whatever your nationality. The basic structure of the garden comprises an upper and a lower level, each with a key feature to provide a focal point. A steel pergola on the upper level, created by artist Simon Packard, frames the garden, softened by the rose, 'Rambling Rector' and provides shade for a variety of foliage plants such as hostas, ferns and rodgersias. A sunken rectangular pond at the centre of the lower level is surrounded by a colourful mass of flowers and foliage, including several varieties of salvias, delphiniums and campanulas, which Foerster introduced. Two interlocking colour themes of blue and white and purple and orange are drawn together by different shades of yellow.

journey of life

" Nature is an infinite sphere of which the centre is everywhere and the circumference nowhere."

Blaise Pascal.

The designer of the "Laurent Perrier Garden" at the RHS Chelsea Flower Show 2007, Jinny Blom, is trained both in theatre design and as a transpersonal psychologist. Though now practising solely as a garden and landscape designer, the Stage and the complexities of the mind can both be seen to influence her work as she plays with perspective and explores the up-lifting effects of a garden upon the human spirit.

This garden is styled to represent part of an imaginary garden attached to the modernist house of an Italian art collector and is inspired by the 'journey of life', offering vistas of the future and a variety of pathways to symbolise the choices we make as we go on our way. The work of the Italian architect Carlo Scarpa is also an influence.

A sculptural progression of circular shapes structures the garden, forming a 'moon gate'. At the entrance, a simple, transparent bronze solar gate invites the visitor in. Beyond, this is echoed by a complex, floating lunar gate suspended above a dark, motionless pond. Marble stepping stones lead over the pond towards a red Italian sandstone disk which forms the dramatic backdrop to a contemplative seat at the end.

Delicate, naturalistic planting in soft, romantic colours, complements the planetary sculptural elements, lending this garden an ethereal quality. A tall hornbeam hedge and candle-shaped fastigiate oaks, planted at the axis of each paving panel, provide a strong foil for the fragility of the planting and add vertical punctuation.

a swedish legacy

" *Plants are upside-down creatures. The roots are their mouths, the leaves are their wings and the flowers their love revealed.* "

Carl Linnaeus.

Thanks to the ubiquitous presence of Swedish furniture brands all over Europe we are familiar with contemporary Swedish style in the home. Swedish style in the garden, however, is less well-known to the public at large. In 'A Tribute to Linnaeus', his garden at the Chelsea Flower Show 2007, Sweden's leading landscape architect, Ulf Nordfjell, presented a coolly elegant design which paid homage to the tercentenary of the 'Father of Taxonomy', Carl Linnaeus, whilst simultaneously revealing his version of Scandinavian garden modernism to a wider audience. The design explores several themes derived from the cultural heritage of Sweden within a stylised interpretation of the country's native woodland landscape. Three bi-coloured timber walls, painted with red iron oxide on one side, the colour of traditional Swedish country homes, and silver grey on the other, representing the 18th century Gustavian period of Linnaeus' time, partially divide the space diagonally. Openings within the walls frame varied views and encourage different ways of looking at the garden.

Water, a dominant feature in the Swedish landscape, appears here in the form of a calm, dark pool where a clump of Linnaeus' beloved golden maidenhair moss grows in a neat circular mound. From the pool, water runs under a granite path to become a fast-flowing stream, flowing over rounded cobbles. Planting is largely restricted to those varieties grown or cultivated by Linnaeus, including the delicately fragrant twinflower, Linnaeus borealis, together with common plants grown in Swedish gardens. The result is a spring-like garden in a simple palette of shades of white and green, intermingled with icy blue and yellow.

" *Every true artist has been inspired more by the beauty of lines and colour and the relationships between them than by the concrete subject of the picture.*"

Piet Mondrian

bold reflections

The early 20th century abstract artist, Mondrian, was the inspiration for Trevor Tooth's "Lloyds TSB Garden" at the RHS Chelsea Flower Show 2007. Grid-like patterns and primary colours were a feature of Mondrian's work and his style is reflected here in a modern, formal design, teamed with a restricted yet vibrant colour palette.

The garden is raised, with a retaining wall clad in black perspex. Floating white steps lead into a lawn area surrounded by abundant planting of trees and shrubs mixed with English perennials selected to complement the green, blue, white and black colour palette. The focal point of the garden is a holographic art panel in blues and greens reflecting onto water to create movement. Two black-lined pools are connected by a narrow rill which divides the plot, separating the verdant, planted area at the front from the paved and covered space designed for relaxation at the rear. Access from one area to the other is via a black glass bridge set at water level to suggest the sensation of walking on water.

on golden pond

" *We are stardust*

We are golden

And we've got to get ourselves

Back to the garden..."

Joni Mitchell "Woodstock".

"Design me a garden for my retirement," was the brief one client gave to Diarmuid Gavin. As yet, the design hasn't been implemented at the client's Surrey home, but it formed the creative basis for 'The Westland Garden', which Gavin exhibited in conjunction with Stephen Reilly, at the Chelsea Flower Show 2007. "On Golden Pond" was an inspiration in the design; an older couple, still in love and still young at heart, enjoying togetherness as the evening sun sinks down over a stretch of water. Reflecting the salad days of the husband and wife who requested the initial design, the garden has that distinctly retro, 1970s feel, which in the 21st century has been absorbed into a style we have come to call 'contemporary'. Its aim is to provide both a stimulating place for each to work – one a writer, the other an artist – and a naturally-inspired, sheltered place in which to rest and relax outdoors. Patterned to form the outlines of giant daisies in another '70s-inspired design allegory, a cobblestone path leads to a large pavilion clad in Western Red Cedar by Irish company, Shomera. Here, adjoining his 'n' hers studios nestle in the shade of woodland planting and overlook a tranquil, natural pond. Planting is mainly evergreen for year-round interest. Varying shades of green are punctuated with splashes of colour, particularly purple, in the form of the allium, 'Purple Sensation', planted prolifically amongst feathery grass, and Monet's graceful iris, springing up all around the pond.

natural exuberance

" *Hope is like a road in the country, there wasn't ever a road, but when many people walk on it, the road comes into existence.* "

Lin Yutang

The power of a garden in bringing people together, to relax, talk and be close to nature, is the essence of Andy Sturgeon's Cancer Research UK Garden at the Chelsea Flower Show 2007, with the charity's vision: "Together we will beat cancer", underpinning the garden's design.

Executed with great lightness of touch, Japanese-inspired, pared down architecture and soft planting creates a tranquil and airy atmosphere. What really lifts this garden to a higher plane however, is a serpentine wooden sculpture which roller-coasters its way through the garden, exuding natural energy and movement. Formed from three ribbons of intertwined steam-bent oak, the 'Together' sculpture creates a series of vistas as it twists and turns, weaving over and through the planting, linking the different elements of the garden to emphasise the message of unity.

Reached via pale walkways of Portuguese limestone, a sunken amphitheatre at the centre of the garden provides a gathering place for a number of people. Resting lightly above the amphitheatre in the dappled shade of the wedding-cake tree Cornus Controversa, is a minimalist, black framed pavilion, inspired by Japanese contemporary architecture, with an acrylic roof and back wall which are illuminated at night. Complementing the Eastern atmosphere of the building, a triptych of smooth ceramic sculptures by Japanese artist Mari-Ruth Oda, hangs on the end wall. The backdrop to the garden is a series of weathered-copper louvers, loosely inspired by the architecture of Richard Seifert, which creates a kaleidoscope of ever-changing shadows throughout the day as the sun moves around. Planting is naturalistic, exuberant and symbolically optimistic, using many shades and textures of green, inter-planted with roses, shrubs and perennials in shades of cerise, pinks, plums and purples. In formal contrast, a series of neatly clipped yew hedges, appearing at different heights to ensure that the entire garden cannot be viewed from any one place, draws the visitor to the centre, presenting a succession of ever-changing vistas along the way.

rooftop escape

"*Your time has come*

open your wings

give the world your colours

don't stay in my hands

I want you

in the blue trees

free

like the day

fly butterfly..."

Carlos Reyes-Manzo, former prisoner of conscience "Oranges in Times of Moon".

Amnesty International were somewhat surprising sponsors of a garden at the Chelsea Flower Show 2007; but challenging the notion of a stereotypical Amnesty supporter is central to the organisation's marketing activity which consistently aims to inform and attract people from all walks of life.

Irish garden designer Paula Ryan collaborated with Artillery Architecture & Interior Design to create "A Garden for Human Rights". Conceived as a roof garden for Amnesty's London headquarters, the design reflects a vision for the world in which every person is born free and equal in dignity and in rights. The concepts of freedom and enclosure are explored in a garden of overlapping terraces, through the juxtaposition of darkness and light and the interplay of vertical and horizontal planes, sight lines and spaces. At one end, a sedum-roofed pavilion shelters a decked terrace, cantilevered over a tranquil pond. Stepping stones lead over the water to the next terrace, enclosed by olive and eucalyptus trees in containers which lend structure, privacy and wind protection to the sunken garden. The lower terrace culminates in a symbolic olive tree.

Planting meets the twin objectives of symbolising Amnesty's mission whilst providing a practical planting solution for an urban roof-top situation. Beneath the clipped trees and prairie-style grasses, perennials in hot colours contrast with the glaucous colours of eucalyptus and echeverias and soften the cityscape. Restraint is balanced with freedom, creating a sustainable retreat to relax the visitor and provide a welcome haven for local birds and insects.

garden of the sun

"*The dream is always*

Midday and the two inheritors are made

Proprietors. They have multiplied the sky.

Where is the water, where the terraces, the Tritons

And the cataracts of moss? This is Australia ..."

Peter Porter "An Australian Garden".

Australian gardens at Chelsea have been an annual event since 2004, bringing their own brand of contemporary outdoor-living to the grounds of the Royal Hospital in London SW3. If one country can be credited with inventing the concept of the outdoor room, it surely must be Australia. In the "Fleming's and Trailfinders' Australian Garden", at the RHS Chelsea Flower Show 2007, Melbourne designer, Mark Browning, presented a strongly architectural and dramatically coloured design for a modern city garden. The main garden area features a raised platform of Australian bluestone under a steel pergola. Planting is dominated by the dusky purple foliage of phormium, beech, heuchera, and other dark plants, which provide contrast to the blue and grey palette of the hard landscaping.

Art plays a prominent role in the garden and takes the form of free-standing sculptures and wall panels, etched to represent the native Australian kangaroo grass. Embedded in the main supporting wall of the pergola, fish tanks promote tranquillity and lend movement to the design of this outdoor room.

mission to mars

"*Aloe, agave, portulaca, prickly pear,*
How these remotely anthropomorphic shapes
Gathered round us in their martian rig...
The eye delighted
In such a weird fair of inflected shapes..."

Chris Wallace-Crabbe "The Life of Ideas".

'600 Days with Bradstone' may not have had the most appealing title for a garden at the Chelsea Flower Show 2007, but its design won the creator, Sarah Eberle, the top award for 'best in show'. The garden is essentially a space fantasy, 'though it is a fantasy created within the realms of scientific possibility, as Sarah spent six years researching how the garden of an astronaut or scientist on a 600 day mission to Mars might function as a place to sustain both body and soul under such 'alien' conditions. Based in an assumed 'Eden-like' geodesic dome, the garden is divided into two interlocking spaces with different functions. The front of the garden is largely connected with food production and planted with vegetables and medicinal plants. A water geyser is used to irrigate the planted areas and forms an attractive fine mist as it emerges from the ground. The rear of the garden, on the other hand, is for relaxation and interaction with the plants to give psychological support. Here, there is a rest pod and hanging seat, and large stone bowls suspended from chains filled with marigolds offer cheerful colour.

Bringing the design back down to earth, the garden offers plenty of ideas for eco-friendly gardening and sustainability in drought conditions. It also demonstrates how selective planting can bring multiple rewards. Sarah's research included identifying varieties which contribute most to the carbon-oxygen cycle; those which 'multi-function' in providing medicine and food; and those that grow quickly and exhibit constant change to alleviate boredom – a concept almost bound to find favour in an impatient and fickle twenty first century.

" *Here may the thoughts expatiate free,*

Embrace that friend, Philosophy,

The jarring crowd forget:

And since those plagues my joys bereave,

With what reluctance here I leave

This happy, blissful seat."

Joseph Giles "The Leasowes".

The Merrill Lynch Garden at the RHS Chelsea Flower Show 2005 was designed by Andy Sturgeon to be an inspiring workplace that is an extension of the home, combining structure and order in hard landscaping with tranquillity and energy derived from water and informal planting.

A modern glass and steel office or studio stands at one end. Grey stone flooring runs away from the building, forming a terrace that cantilevers over a striking black pool of still water, created by architectural metalwork specialists, Tadpole, which is the centrepiece of the garden. Square holes cut through the water's mirrored surface create mysterious voids.

Structural planting of trees and shrubs provides background colour to the garden, ranging from bright green to very dark green. Against this backdrop, a blend of exotic and native varieties forms a colourful carpet under a copse of dainty leaved birch trees, and a river of grasses, punctuated by dark purple Tulipa 'Queen of the Night', flows the length of the garden, creating soft movement.

The calming influence of the water is best appreciated from the vantage point of the small hillock rising at one end of the terrace. Here, echoing the dark voids of the pool is a series of multi-functional oak cubes which appear first as seats on the terrace, then 'morph' to become steps floating above and through clumps of iris and Inula, before finally forming a path which leads through the plants and along the water.

"*In these ways one gets to know how to use colour to the best garden effects. It is a kind of optical gastronomy; this preparation and presentation of food for the eye in arrangements that are both wholesome and agreeable, and in which each course is so designed that it is the best possible preparation for the next one to come.*"

Gertrude Jekyll, Home and Garden 1900.

In her "Naturally Fresh" garden at Bloom 2007, landscape architect Jane McCorkell presented a contemporary version of the old-fashioned potager, marrying fruit and vegetable production with herbaceous planting in the context of a luxurious and coolly styled outdoor room. The garden was designed for a professional couple who would not only want to relax in their garden but enjoy spending time tending to its varied and seasonal needs. Design inspiration came from the large scale production and distribution of fruit, vegetables and flowers by sponsors, Keelings. Conveyor belts laden with fruit for inspection are reflected in the rectilinear theme of the garden and an abundance of water is a key presence in its design, symbolising the life-giving and cleansing roles of water in food production.

The garden stretches out before a raised seating area, furnished with an inviting tangerine-cushioned sofa in teak and stainless steel and decorated with a trio of acid-etched glass panels, each depicting a different fruit. Behind, an L-shaped red cedar fence makes a richly toned backdrop, with elegant pleached pears and box hedging planted in front and the tapering spires of the white foxglove, Digitalis 'Snow Thimble', swaying in its shadows.

Running from mixed rows of fruit and vegetables, where scarlet-flowered runner beans climb eagerly skywards with strawberries, scallions and salad leaves at their feet, a quietly flowing stream of water makes its way through the garden, passing the lawn with its giant Bathstone apple and rising now and again as fountains, foaming with restrained exuberance, before arriving finally where an apple tree stands ahead of a profusion of informally planted summer flowers.

" *Show me your garden and I shall tell you*
what you are."

Alfred Austin

Elma Fenton's work first grabbed the headlines at the Chelsea Flower Show in 2005 where her design: "Moat and Castle Eco-Garden", incorporated Chelsea's first ever natural swimming pond.

At Bloom 2007, the lynchpin of Elma's garden once again, was a tranquil, curving swimming pond, its hour-glass shape bordered with oak decking, cantilevered over the water's surface to soften the pool's outline and reinforce the connection between two natural materials. The natural pool is self-cleaning, with filtration occurring organically through appropriate planting without the need for chemicals, allowing the user to swim in water as nature intended. In this design, areas of loose Donegal quartz stone have been deposited around the plants at the water's edge where they act to collect debris and encourage settlement.

Show me your garden and
I'll tell you who you are

The over-riding inspiration of the garden is a desire to deliver an ecologically sustainable design, yet it has been planned to work as a place of relaxation and entertainment with shaded rest and eating areas as well as all the "required elements" of the urban garden, combining lawn, decked and paved areas. Planting is largely composed of luscious green aquatic varieties necessary for filtration, yet these are interspersed with splashes of colour and texture, from the little bog cotton with its fluffy white seed heads, to the blue of the water forget-me-not and the warm orange of a clump of candelabra primulas situated in a sunny spot next to the pale terracotta tone of the garden wall.

A wholly natural garden such as this demands little in the way of ornamentation and Elma chose simply to add subtle details, such as a sculpture suggesting the shapes of sailing boats blown across the water, and hand-blown purple glass objets, like glistening aubergines, placed against the white quartz filling of brushed steel planters to add another hint of colour.

perfect proportions

" *Not wholly in the busy world, nor quite*

Beyond it, blooms the garden that I love.

News from the humming city comes to it...

...And, sitting muffled in dark leaves, you hear..."

Alfred, Lord Tennyson "Suburban Garden".

In the 'Orchard Home & Garden' at Bloom 2007, Paul Martin demonstrated how the standard design elements of paving, grass and water could be combined in an area measuring only 8m x 10m to produce a tranquil outdoor room for contemporary city living. The garden has been designed with the square metre as a basic building block to lend consistency and symmetry. At the entrance, square box bushes are planted in gravel either side of a black terrazzo path alongside drifts of blue agapanthus. The path leads to a raised terrazzo terrace, complete with chic black and white furniture, which overlooks an L-shaped lawn area at the centre of the garden. A series of painted walls teamed with architectural planting unveil a succession of changing views, keeping the overall design a secret from the visitor. Parallel to the path, across the garden, a long, metre-wide canal is fed by water cascading down a stainless steel wall. Planting at the water's edge arches over the pool where Koi Carp glide under its reflective surface. At right angles to the head of the canal two sculptural green walls have been positioned as a backdrop, with elongated windows cut through to provide a glimpse of golden bamboo which is up-lit at night.

blossoming bright

"*Here in this sequestered close*
Bloom the hyacinth and rose;
Here, beside the modest stock
Flaunts the flaring hollyhock;
Here, without a pang, one sees
Ranks, conditions, and degrees."

Henry Austin Dobson "A Garden Song: to W.E.H."

The plant displays of the Great Pavilion at the RHS Chelsea Flower Show are for many, the highlight of this annual event. Protected from the elements by a vast marquee, prized exhibits of flowers, foliage and vegetables from nurseries, growers and plant specialists the world over, combine to assault the senses, presenting explosions of colour at every turn while the air is filled with a heady fragrance from thousands of blooms. These spectacular displays are the outcome of years of painstaking work, during which time the plantsmen have battled to nurture each variety, so that on 'show day' every specimen, however out-of-season, will be as close to perfection as possible. Chelsea is also the venue of choice to launch new varieties to the public after development lead-times which can last a decade or more.

Intermingling with floral specialists are verdant stands such as that belonging to The Romantic Garden Nursery who presented 'A Cabinet de Verdure', at Chelsea 2007, a formal garden designed by George Carter.

Here, a trio of lead obelisk fountains is surrounded by beds planted with topiary, including laxus, prunus and buxus balls. Short-stemmed pleached carpinus trees enclose the centre and a selection of small buxus topiary makes up the outer edge, in-filled with lavender.

'Water is precious for health, for wealth and for life itself', was the theme of the Gateshead Council and Northumbrian Water garden at the Chelsea Flower Show 2007, which was an eye-catching three-dimensional display using a mass of bedding plants and perennials. A large, stylised globe represents the beginning of the water cycle whereby water flows from the North Pole of the globe and is pumped through the centre to repeat the cycle. Beneath this centrepiece, the health benefits of water are represented through common plants with medicinal benefits. These plants give way to water thirsty and exotic planting to represent the way we take water for granted. At the outer limits of the garden is an area of desertification with drought tolerant plants to represent climate change and the after-effects of a water-thirsty existence.

gardens with a story to tell

emerald treasure

"*It is said that once a man has seen Venice he is filled with longing to see it again, and that exactly describes what must occur with every horticultural enthusiast who sees Mount Usher.*"

FW Millard.

The magnificent twenty acre garden at Mount Usher Mill near Ashford in County Wicklow stands in the sheltered valley of the Vartry River as it flows down from the Devil's Glen. A perfectly preserved example of a Victorian, 'Robinsonian' garden, its survival into the 21st century is thanks to the devotion of its long-time custodian, Mrs Madelaine Jay.

Wrapped in a blanket of trees and occupying what is said to be the site of an old lake, this "gardened demesne" is blessed with its own micro climate and a fertile, alluvial soil, which enables an enormous variety of semi-exotic trees and shrubs to thrive outdoors, unpunished by the northerly latitude. The Vartry runs the length of the garden, spilling over a series of weirs and passing under suspension bridges which allow the visitor to cross backwards and forwards haphazardly to enjoy the delights of Mount Usher as it was intended, for this was a garden which grew intuitively, without a plan.

Five generations of the Walpole family originated and then developed the garden in line with the teaching of William Robinson, who denounced formal planting and advocated that trees and shrubs should be allowed to grow naturally. Dublin businessman Edward Walpole first took out a lease on the mill in 1868, planting a garden in place of the old potato patch and then in 1875 transferred his interest in the property to his three sons, Thomas, George and Edward, for whom the garden became a passion.

Sir Frederick Moore, Curator of the Botanic Gardens in Glasnevin, described the brothers at work: "To this delightful garden the Walpoles came from Saturday to Monday during eight to nine months of the year. Each had his own particular work … Edward's armament consisting of a trowel and a secateur; George, being less energetic, took charge of the plant book and labels, and made notes. Before any important change was made there was a consultation, Thomas taking part, and unanimity was arrived at after friendly but full discussion." In 1917, the gardens passed on to Edward Horace Walpole, the son of Edward Walpole junior, who acquired the freehold and demolished the old mill house, replacing it with the house which stands on "the Island" today. On his death in 1964, his only son, Robert Walpole, inherited Mount Usher and lived there until mounting costs forced him to sell in 1980. Following the departure of the last Walpole from Mount Usher, the gardens passed into the custodianship of Mrs Madelaine Jay who has ensured their safe passage into the twenty first century. The story of how a Swiss American with no interest in gardening came to devote almost a third of her life to ensuring the survival of this unique landscape is one for which Ireland is deeply grateful.

Madelaine Röntgen was born in Zurich in 1921 to American parents of German and Scottish extraction. They had apparently found early twentieth century America 'rather tedious' and consequently took off for Europe, settling for a time in the Swiss city of Zurich.

Her mother, she says, 'was mad about gardening' and put a good deal of energy into the garden at their house in the country. The young Madelaine, on the other hand, couldn't have cared less about horticulture; as far as she was concerned there were too many dull chores associated with its pursuit. Her passion was for horses. Recognising that she had a talent worth nurturing, Madelaine's mother sent her to the cavalry school in Hanover where she spent the winter being taught to ride by a Prussian officer she remembers as "quite formidable, yet wonderful". It was at the cavalry school where she first came across a dashing young cavalry officer who teased her when she sought his permission to ride; his name was Hans Jay. It would be another 15 years before they saw each other again. Hans went off to war and was eventually captured by the Allied Forces when they stormed into a capitulating Paris. After some time as a POW in Canada, he was sent to a camp in England where he volunteered to take on work outside the camp (officers were not obliged to work) and found himself as a gardener in the temporary employ of a vicar and his wife. He knew nothing about gardening, his life had been the army and his horses, but the vicar's wife taught him about plants and how to care for them. When the time came for all POWs to be repatriated or sent on to a place they had connections with, Hans was sent to Ireland where he had often been to buy horses for the Army before the War. Meanwhile, Madelaine was completing her studies in Switzerland and her mother decided that she should take a break and go to Ireland to hunt, duly despatching her to stay in the care of a family friend, the colourful Swiss officer, Colonel Eric Miville, at Ballykeane House near Redcross in County Wicklow. It was here that she once again came across Colonel Hans Jay.

They married in 1952 and moved to a farm in Kildare where they trained horses and raised cattle. All was well, despite the house being the coldest place Madelaine said she had ever stayed in, until the early '70s when the political situation caused her husband to become disillusioned with his adopted country. Although Madelaine wanted to stay, as she loved Ireland, they made plans to return to Switzerland. But then Hans died suddenly – he was much older than Madelaine – and with him perished any desire she had to return to Switzerland. For a few years Madelaine continued to manage the farm but eventually realised that farming alone was not to her taste.

Some time previously, an English friend had talked about the wonderful gardens at Mount Usher. Madelaine was interested but thought no more about them until by chance at a dinner party she overheard that the estate was for sale. She went to view and fell in love with the place. Encouraged by her accountant, Russell Murphy, she put the farm up for sale and purchased Mount Usher. This was 1980; Madelaine Jay was 59 years old and a widow with a young son; she also had no experience in managing a 20 acre garden open to the public.

The next twenty seven years were spent battling to preserve the gardens and raise the income required for their survival. A pivotal role has been that of head gardener. For the first two years Madelaine was fortunate to have the guiding hand of Mr Walpole's Head Gardener, Myles "Miley" Manning, who had worked at Mount Usher for 40 years. Since his departure in 1982, Mrs Jay has worked with several head gardeners, most latterly Sean Heffernan, the current incumbent. During this time she has developed a fundamental understanding of the garden and how the Walpoles conceived it: "I still don't know the plant names," she confesses, "but I have an instinct about what suits the garden and what doesn't."

Editor's note: In 2007, at the age of 86, Madelaine Jay handed over the running of Mount Usher gardens and courtyard shops to Avoca Handweavers, owned by the Pratt family.

true to nature

" *You see, sweet maid, we marry*

A gentler scion to the wildest stock,

And make conceive a bark of baser kind

By bud nobler race: this is an art

Which does mend Nature: change it rather: but

The art itself is Nature."

William Shakespeare.

Gentlemen in Black Tie and ladies in silken evening gowns still sip cocktails on balmy summer evenings in the garden at Gravetye Manor, just as they did over a century ago, as guests of William Robinson. Today, Gravetye Manor is an immensely comfortable Relais & Chateaux country house hotel, set in magnificent grounds nestling in the undulating countryside of West Sussex. It's a much-loved resting place for many who don formal eveningwear and make the annual summer pilgrimage to the world-famous opera festival at near-by Glyndebourne. But between 1884 and 1935 Gravetye Manor was the home of William Robinson, an Irishman, of whom unfairly little has been written, yet who was arguably the most influential gardener of the late nineteenth and early twentieth centuries. The thirty acres of grounds at the hotel do a great deal to enhance the visitor's stay at Gravetye's Elizabethan manor house. In quintessential English country hotel style, guests can always expect a welcoming log fire and afternoon tea on the lawn and the 'entertainment' is peace and quiet and blissful surroundings. There's neither spa here, nor golf course and holiday cottages, for the thousand acre Gravetye Estate was left by Robinson to the State for forestry cultivation, whilst the manor house and its gardens are privately owned by co-directors Andrew Russell and Mark Raffan. They have worked at the hotel for almost 20 years and see it very much as their duty to preserve the "grand old man's" garden for future generations, continuing a tradition established by their predecessor, Peter Herbert, who rescued the house and garden from the decay of the War Years.

"Fate gave me a piece of land in which all had to be done," wrote Robinson when he bought Gravetye in July 1885. How a poor lad from County Down in Northern Ireland came to create a world famous garden in the grounds of a prestigious manor house and thousand acre estate in the south east of England, is a remarkable story.

Little is known of Robinson's early years, although there is plenty of speculation. It is said that his father, a land agent, had deserted his wife and young family in famine-stricken Ireland, and run off to America with Lady St George, the wife of his employer. Growing up without a father, Robinson was forced to work for a living at an early age, beginning his career at Curraghmore, the Marquess of Waterford's estate, before becoming a student gardener at the National Botanic Garden in Glasnevin, Dublin. Legend has Robinson labelled as a bad-tempered and rather unpleasant individual. Although there is much evidence to the contrary, the foundation of this characterisation probably dates from his time in the employment of the Walsh family at Ballykilcavan in Stradbally, County Laois. In the winter of 1860-1, Robinson is thought to have had a serious falling-out with the head gardener at Ballykilcavan. He departed on the spot and walked to Dublin through the night, leaving the greenhouses unattended. This much was recounted by a Walsh family member, but the story has been embellished over time and Robinson is not only rumoured to have deserted the greenhouses but extinguished all the fires and opened the windows, leaving his delicate charges to perish in the harsh winter frosts. Whatever really happened, the incident ultimately had a positive outcome in furthering Robinson's career as he soon left Ireland to work at the Royal Botanic Society's garden at Regent's Park in London. Here he became a key member of staff and as time went on, was drawn into an influential circle which included Charles Darwin. Whilst at Regent's Park, Robinson began the writing career that would bring him both fame and fortune. In 1866, Robinson resigned from his position to devote himself full-time to horticultural literature. After publishing several gardening books, including "The Wild Garden", in 1871 he launched a successful magazine, "The Garden", followed by "Gardening Illustrated" in 1879, which was immediately snapped up by a garden-loving public, enjoying a weekly circulation in excess of 30,000. Gertrude Jekyll was amongst the contributors to Robinson's magazines and having like-minded views on gardening, the two developed a strong and lasting friendship. Running his own magazines not only brought financial rewards but gave Robinson the freedom to air his passionately held, often controversial, views on gardening.

He despised formal gardening and particularly hated the system of 'bedding-out' whereby hundreds of the same types of plants would be laid out to produce patterns – "pastry-cook's gardening" – he called it. Robinson's favoured style was for a natural and yet, adventurous garden, and in his most famous and influential publication, "The English Flower Garden", he wrote that: "…the aim being to make the garden a reflex of the beauty of the great garden of the world itself, and to prove that the true way to happiest design is not to have any stereotyped style for all flower gardens, but that the best kind of garden should arise out of its site and conditions as happily as a primrose out of a cool bank".

By 1885, Robinson was a wealthy man, having profitably invested his income from publishing in the City and property. In July of this year, he was reading "The Times" and came across an advertisement for: "a singularly attractive and highly valuable residential property, distinguished (since XVI century) and known as Gravetye Manor Estate …" A mere month later, on the 24th August, Robinson began to tackle the then 360 acres of the Gravetye Manor Estate. Over the next 50 years, Robinson transformed not only the gardens of the old manor house, but also the surrounding countryside. For eventually he came to own around 1,000 acres of the land around Gravetye, much of which he planted with trees. Mea Allan says in her biography of Robinson: "Seen from afar you can tell where Gravetye lies, for in no other woodland around is there such beauty of grouping, such contrasts of leaf-colour." Between 1889 and 1890, Robinson planted some 120,000 trees of all kinds. Closer to the house, whilst he devoted his flower garden, the West Garden, almost completely to the cultivation of some of his favourite flowers – tea roses, carnations, pansies and starworts (Robinson's name for Michaelmas Daisies), he also worked on a series of other gardens – the East Garden, bordering the drive, with its camellias and rhododendrons, the Wild Garden on the banks above the house with its collection of hardy exotics and then the Alpine Meadow which runs down to the Lower Lake, which he planted with drifts of the blue Appenine anemone he had seen on his travels in Greece. One of his greatest achievements in the garden, the kitchen garden or fruit garden as he called it, is still under cultivation today, growing fruit, flowers and vegetables for use in the hotel within the great oval wall of stone Robinson had constructed, the theory being that its curved walls would ensure that the frost had no corner to settle in.

Robinson's initials are still there in the kitchen garden, "W.R." carved above a stone bench, half-hidden beneath the cascading branches of an aged mulberry tree. Life changed dramatically for the still sprightly Robinson in 1909, when aged 71 he suffered a fall on his way to church, injuring his back. Afterwards he was confined to bed, unable to walk and later it was confirmed that he would never walk again as his fall had caused the insidious syphilis he was unaware of, to flare up, bringing sudden paralysis. To his utter dismay, without his active intervention and guiding hand, for he could only visit in his wheelchair, the garden at Gravetye began to show signs of decline. Salvation arrived in 1910 in the form of a new head gardener, Ernest Markham, and under his influence the gardens were given renewed vigour. Like Robinson, Markham was a clematis enthusiast, and together they cultivated over 60 varieties, some of which are named in their honour, such as Clematis taxensis 'Gravetye Beauty' and Clematis 'Earnest Markham'. On his 95th birthday, the headlines in the London Evening News read: "He changed the face of England. Grand old man of the new gardening. Flowers his life's love." On 12th May 1935, William Robinson died. Things were in a sorry state at Gravetye when Peter Herbert arrived in 1957. He had the then revolutionary idea of transforming the old house and garden into a country house hotel. People thought it was madness to site a luxury hotel and restaurant 30 miles from London, hidden away in a wooded enclave. But Herbert persisted with his plans and succeeded in creating a famous hotel with a renowned kitchen. As for the garden, he turned to Robinson's own record of its development: "Twenty years work around a manor house", using it as his bible to restore the legendary gardener's creation. Almost 50 years on, the restoration work is still in progress to this day, such were the extent and complexity of the gardens. In private hands, Gravetye does not enjoy lottery funding or other such financial benefits to aid its restoration, but little by little projects are completed (such as the recent restoration of the peach house, for instance) and a remarkable garden moves one step closer to its glorious past.

Much of the history of William Robinson related here has been gleaned from Mea Allen's excellent biography: "William Robinson 1838-1935 Father of the English Flower Garden".

rose garden

"*Climbing roses had run all over ... and swung down long tendrils which made light swaying curtains, and here and there they had caught at each other or at a far-reaching branch and had crept from one tree to another and made lovely bridges of themselves...*"

Frances Hodgson Burnett "The Secret Garden".

Kiftsgate Court is often described as a very English garden, renowned for that symbol of English gardening, the rose. A decade away from celebrating the centenary of its creation, the garden has always been tended by the same family whose consistent influence has imparted a special intimacy to these exuberantly cultivated acres. From the middle of June to early July, the famous Rose Garden at Kiftsgate is at its stunning best, the romantic ideal of the English garden. Yet of course, the cultivated 'English rose' isn't English at all, as Vita Sackville-West pointed out in verse "…The young Crusaders found the Syrian rose/Springing from Saracenic quoins,/ And China opened her shut gate/To let her roses through, and Persian shrines/Of poetry and painting gave the rose…".

One such Chinese escapee has for almost 80 years been thriving in this particular corner of the thoroughly anglicised Cotswolds to become one of the world's most famous roses – Rosa filipes 'Kiftsgate'. This most vigorous of ramblers was identified by the great plantsman and garden writer, Graham Stuart Thomas, when he visited Kiftsgate Court in 1951. It is now thought to be the largest rose in England and when last measured, sized up at a colossal 80ft × 90ft × 50ft high. Bought in 1938 as a Rosa moschata, Thomas saw that it was in fact a filipes rose from the wilds of China and applied to the RHS to have it formally named after the place he had discovered it to be growing. Roses, however, are just one of the delightful pleasures to be found in these gardens. Situated close to the picturesque Gloucestershire village of Chipping Campden, Kiftsgate occupies an elevated and fertile site on an escarpment overlooking the Vale of Evesham. Sharing this rich seam of soil, a mere five minutes walk away, is the UK's most famous garden, Hidcote Manor, created by Major Lawrence Johnston in the early 1900s and now run by the National Trust.

Both can loosely be described as 'Arts and Crafts' gardens, but whilst Hidcote is all about magnificent vistas and geometrical design, Kiftsgate is an altogether more intimate garden, exquisitely planted and lovingly tended, with a softer, more feminine feel. And unlike Hidcote, which is undergoing a massive restoration programme to return it to Johnston's original vision after decades of change under succeeding head gardeners, Kiftsgate has managed to keep its identity, having always been gardened by one family with a shared vision. The feminine atmosphere at the garden of Kiftsgate Court might just have something to do with the fact that it has been created and sustained by women of the same family for three generations since the early twentieth century. Anne Chambers is the third generation and current custodian of the house and gardens which she has been running with her husband Johnny since 1990. It was Anne's grandmother, Heather Muir, who first settled here, coming to live at Kiftsgate in 1918, not to create a garden but primarily to avail of the excellent hunting in the surrounding area. Around a decade earlier, Johnston had moved into Hidcote Manor, and by the time the Muirs arrived, was already ensconced in an obsession of garden creation which would take over his life. The two neighbours became firm friends and Johnston encouraged Mrs Muir to do something more with the garden at Kiftsgate, which at that time comprised only a formal paved garden in front of the portico, with a grass field and wooded banks beyond. By the early 1930s much had been accomplished. The areas surrounding the house had been laid out and the Yellow and Wide borders planted. Hedges and paths were in place and the steep wooded banks had begun to be tackled. Italian gardeners terraced them and a summer house was built with steps descending to a lawn below. Seized and delighted by this new past-time, the erstwhile reluctant gardener continued with her work and by the end of the War period, Heather Muir's cautious beginnings had been nurtured and transformed into a masterful and luxuriant tapestry of colour. So much so, in fact, that when Graham Stuart Thomas visited he wrote afterwards in the RHS journal: "I regard this as the finest piece of skilled colour work that it has been my pleasure to see".

Diany Binny, Anne Chambers' mother, took over the running of the garden at about this time and Heather moved into the Front Lodge. Inheriting her mother's talents for plant and colour selection, Diany continued the nourishment and development of the garden and it was she who began to help fund its upkeep by opening regularly to a paying public. Whilst the form of the garden essentially remained as her mother had laid it out, Diany made her mark too with additions such as the half moon swimming pool in the Lower Garden and the pool and fountain in the White Sunk Garden close to the house. She also commissioned two stone sculptures – Mother and Child and Seated Lady – by Simon Verity, an artist influenced by the Arts and Crafts tradition. Some forty years later history repeated itself with Diany moving into the Front Lodge and Anne and her husband leaving London to devote their energies to Kiftsgate. Whilst Heather Muir employed five full-time gardeners, the Chambers have only two who take care of sections of the workload; the rest they do themselves. But this is how the garden remains consistent, according to Anne: "We are the head gardeners; we make all the decisions about the garden and do all the planting. It's not a question of not trusting anyone else but rather that it has to be this way to keep the personality of the garden, because, naturally, everyone has their own ideas."

Consistency doesn't have to mean an end to evolution, though. Plants reach the end of their natural lives and need replacement and there are areas of the garden still under development, such as the Banks that Anne's grandmother had terraced in the 1930s. Here the Chambers continue to experiment with exotics and sub-tropical varieties that can survive in the sheltered conditions lower down. But whilst visitors are blissfully unaware of the Chambers' relentless work in maintaining the garden, they will all leave remembering the couple's most visible contribution to Kiftsgate, namely, the Water Garden.

Kiftsgate closes during the winter for essential maintenance and back in the winter of 1999, the Chambers decided that they should create something in the garden to mark the Millennium. The solution came in the form of the old tennis court, built in the 1930s and enclosed with high yew hedging, which had fallen into disuse. Having long contemplated how more water could be introduced to the garden – as Kiftsgate doesn't have a stream – they came up with the idea of replacing the tennis court with a water garden. In complete contrast to the rest of the landscape, the Water Garden is a modernist, Zen-like enclosure where a motionless inky black pool, edged in white Portland Stone, sits within high yew walls, bordered by strips of lawn. At one end, precision-cut stone steps lead out to a grassed platform and at the other, sculptor Simon Allison's delicate water feature makes a stunning focal point as twenty-four stainless steel stems topped with gilded bronze philodendron leaves glisten and sway gently in the breeze. Despite the dramatic departure in style from the rest of the garden, the Water Garden still feels 'right'; an early twenty first century addition to add new interest to an early twentieth century garden. Wrapped in its blanket of yew the garden doesn't encroach upon any other vista in the garden but rather, sits tranquilly, waiting to be discovered. As to whether there will be a fourth female generation of the family at Kiftsgate who will come along and make their own special mark, we shall have to wait and see: "We have never assumed that our children would take over the garden," says Anne. In the meantime, the garden and England's most famous rose remain a national treasure – in the safest of hands.

Kiftsgate Court Garden is open to the public between April and September.

great expectations

"*She was dressed in rich materials – satins, and lace, and silks – all of white. Her shoes were white. And she had a long white veil dependent from her hair, and she had bridal flowers in her hair, but her hair was white...*

...the garden of the house... was overgrown with tangled weeds ... there was a track upon the green and yellow paths, as if someone sometimes walked there..."

Charles Dickens "Great Expectations".

With its neatly clipped box hedging and tidy-minded symmetry, architect Alfred Cochrane's garden at Corke Lodge near Shankill, County Dublin, is a far cry from the decay and chaos of Miss Haversham's garden in Dickens' "Great Expectations", yet there is a connection, both historical and spiritual. The garden fans out around the rear of the house and Cochrane has designed it with an architect's eye. Immediately visible are the lines of sight he has created through different planting arrangements. It's a verdant garden, relying on texture and form for interest, rather than a proliferation of coloured blossoms. Yet despite first impressions, the garden of Corke Lodge is not merely a garden of formality, but one filled with eccentricities and surprises, wherein beats a romantic and wild heart. A short walk down a lush green 'allee', passing a clipped 'parterre', plunges the visitor quickly into dark woodland, where tangled pockets of wilderness have been encouraged to flourish, deliberately symbolising how formality is easily overcome by nature's rebellious ways and as an ever-green homage to the many grand gardens which suffered the same fate as Miss Haversham's. Cochrane has been inspired in the idiosyncratic design of his garden in part by the history of the house and its previous owners. It is said that Dickens' own inspiration for his tragic character, Miss Haversham, was the one-time proprietor of Corke Lodge, Augusta Magan. One of the richest women in nineteenth century Ireland, and owner of many properties, Augusta chose to live as a recluse at No. 77 St. Stephen's Green in Dublin city centre. Legend has it that when the house was sold following her death, a wedding dress was discovered and the dining room was laid as if for a celebration.

Dating from the early 1800s, Corke Lodge is a delightfully whimsical building, with a classical façade and gothic rear elevation, and was clearly intended to be a romantic seaside retreat for the Magans. The likelihood is that it was designed by the architect, William Farrell, who also designed Clonearl, the family's country house in County Offaly, together with the nearby church at Crinken. The Magans planted the original garden as a 'pleasure ground' in the fashionable 'Mediterranean' style, much favoured by the grand houses in Killiney; and so one finds sequoias, American cedars and evergreen oaks as well as a magnificently gnarled cork oak, planted because its leaves were felt to resemble those of the olive. After Augusta's death, Corke Lodge was absorbed into the neighbouring estate of Woodbrook, owned by the eccentric Sir Stanley Cochrane (the present owner's great uncle), the heir to the mineral water fortune of Cantrell & Cochrane. A great lover and patron of both sport and the arts he installed a cricket ground and golf course on the estate and built his own opera house, where the great soprano Nellie Melba came to sing and which was the origination of Glyndebourne. Until Alfred Cochrane inherited Corke Lodge upon the death of his father in 1980, the house had been mostly vacant, apart from a period in the 1950s when it was leased to Geraldine Fitzgerald of Ardmore Studios, and the likes of Catherine Hepburn came to stay. By the 1980s, both house and garden were in a woeful state; the trees that in their youth evoked an Italianate illusion had completely encroached upon the house, causing its partial collapse. Alfred set about restoring the Corke Lodge and creating a garden out of the gloomy wilderness he had inherited. He decided to retain the gothic appearance of the back of the house and purchased a large quantity of salvage material from the demolition of Glendalough House, the Tudor Revival mansion built for the Barton family by Daniel Robinson and the former home of President Childers. What he didn't use in the house, he put to work in the garden.

As a result, remnants of gothic architecture present themselves all over the two acre plot, looming at the end of dark, wooded paths and arranged like monastic remains amongst drought-tolerant plants in a new 'Mediterranean' garden where the sun falls upon a pair of elegant white chaise longues designed by Eileen Gray for Sir Stanley's turkish bath at Woodbrook House. A micro-climate created by the encircling trees has meant that a great variety of sub-tropical trees and shrubs have flourished; some of which were in the garden originally, such as a large Chilean Myrtle, Miss Haversham's bridal flower, its rusty-barked stems twisting and turning under the blanket of delicate white blossoms above, and others which have been given as gifts by friends, such as the hoherias. Previous gardeners have also been influential in shaping the garden, leaving their mark in the form of fine trees, such as the elegant specimen from Chatham Island growing close to the house which was a gift from Diarmuid Gavin, a former gardener at Corke Lodge. Cochrane also recalls an eccentric Englishman who worked for him for a number of years and used to bring plants from the smart gardens he tended all over Dublin. Returning to the house in a loop, one passes down an avenue of tall cordylines which direct another interesting vista out into the garden. They were planted by Cochrane as a symbolic reminder of his childhood home in the Lebanon. He says, smiling, that they might be considered rather "naff" by some of his distinguished garden friends in the Dublin Gardens Group, but concludes and is consoled by the fact that in Miss Haversham's day they would have been exotically acceptable.

garden directory

gardens

Bodnant Garden:

One of the world's most spectacular gardens, Bodnant Garden is situated above the River Conwy, with stunning views across Snowdonia. Begun in 1875, Bodnant Garden is the creation of four generations of Aberconways and features huge Italianate terraces and formal lawns on its upper level, with a wooded valley, stream and wild garden below.

There are dramatic colours throughout the season, with fine collections of rhododendrons, magnolias and camellias in early spring. The spectacular laburnum arch is a 55yd tunnel of golden blooms from mid-May to early June. Herbaceous borders, roses, hydrangeas, water lilies and clematis delight throughout the summer, with superb autumn colours during October.

Bodnant Garden, Tal-y-Cafn, Colwyn Bay, Conwy, LL28 5RE,
t: +44 1492 650460
bodnantgarden@nationaltrust.org.uk
www.nationaltrust.org.uk

Calke Abbey:

Informal pleasure grounds and parkland provide the stunning setting for the baroque mansion at Calke Abbey. The parkland is kept as a nature conservation area, while a beautiful walled garden including a flower garden and physic garden can be found in the grounds.

Throughout the season the flower garden is resplendent with colour and texture. The intricate geometric layout, dominated by Chusan Palms, is a kaleidoscope of colour. The beds brim with wallflowers in spring. In summer, roses, clematis and wisteria that cling to the walls.

The walled garden, formerly the Physic Garden, is now managed as a kitchen garden with sweet scents that pervade the air. Dating from the 18th century, the garden was created for the cultivation of medicinal herbs and plants. Today, it still provides fresh herbs to the restaurant in the stable block.

Calke Abbey, Ticknell, Derbyshire, DE73 7LE
t: +44 1332 863822 or calkeabbey@nationaltrust.org.uk
www.nationaltrust.org.uk

Hidcote Manor Garden:

One of the England's great gardens, Hidcote dates from the early years of the 20th century, when the Arts & Crafts movement was in its full flowering. Hidcote consists of a series of outdoor rooms, separated by hedging of boxwood, yew, holly and hornbeam. It was created from 1907 onwards by Lawrence Johnston, a superb plantsman and horticulturist.

Each 'room' has a unique character and colour scheme. Many rare shrubs and trees, outstanding herbaceous borders, old roses and unusual plant varieties can be savoured at Hidcote, some of which were developed here. The range of plants used by Johnston was huge - in a never-ending quest, he secured rare and exotic species by sponsoring and actually taking part in plant hunting expeditions.

Hidcote Manor Garden, Hidcote Bartrim, Chipping Campden, Glous, GL55 6LR
t: +44 1386 483333 or hidcote@nationaltrust.org.uk
www.nationaltrust.org.uk

Mount Stewart Garden:

The famous gardens at Mount Stewart were planted in the 1920s by Edith, Lady Londonderry, and have been nominated a World Heritage Site. The magnificent series of outdoor 'rooms' and vibrant parterres contain many rare plants that thrive in the mild climate of the Ards Peninsula. There are dramatic views over Strangford Lough from the Temple of the Winds (based on the Tower of the Winds in Athens).

In early summer the Sunken Garden is ablaze with vivid orange and yellow when the azaleas reach their peak and the scarlet blooms of the Red Hand of Ulster in the Shamrock Garden are equally splendid.

In high summer the Italian garden comes into its own with its magnificent array of roses and herbaceous plants in symmetrical beds.

Mount Stewart Garden, Portaferry Road, Newtownards, County Down, BT22 2AD, t: +44 2842 788387
mountstewart@nationaltrust.org.uk
www.nationaltrust.org.uk

Mount Usher:

The Robinsonian style Mount Usher gardens laid out along the banks of the River Vartry offers varying pleasures at different seasons of the year. Rhododendrons in Spring, a blaze of Summer colour and the wistful tints of Autumn, all elegantly set off by the crystal waters of the river. In Spring, bulbs will be in full bloom along the Palm Walk and the air full of the scent of magnolia and cherry blossom. We believe that the serenity and natural beauty that epitomise Mount Usher is perfect as somewhere to do nothing more than "time out".

Mount Usher truly manages to prove itself as being an ideal spot for a family day out, catching up with friends or simply escaping the hustle and bustle of the city.

t: +353 404 40205 or +353 87 230 1678
www.mountushergardens.ie

Nymans Garden:

Nymans is one of the great gardens of the Sussex Weald and is internationally famous for its beauty and collection of rare plants. It is the achievement of three generations of the Messel family over a period of over a hundred years. Nymans was one of the first gardens to come to the English National Trust when it was bequeathed into its care in 1953. The inspiring fusion of garden styles incorporates a stunning spring display and knock-out summer borders. Nymans is a 'theatrical' garden full of variety, surprises and delight. There are wonderful views over the Sussex countryside towards the South Downs. A fire in 1947 destroyed much of the house, but the ruins form a romantic backdrop to the garden. The 275 acres of woodland include walks, a conifer avenue and lake.

Nymans Garden, Handcross, Haywards Heath, West Sussex, RH17 6EB
t: +44 1444 405250 or nymans@nationaltrust.org.uk
www.nationaltrust.org.uk

Powerscourt Gardens:

One of the world's great gardens situated 20km South of Dublin in the foothills of the Wicklow mountains. The gardens were begun by Richard Wingfield, Viscount Powerscourt, in the 1740s. The word garden belies the magnitude of this creation which stretches out over 47 acres. It is a sublime blend of formal gardens, sweeping terraces, statuary and ornamental lakes together with secret hollows, rambling walks, walled gardens and over 200 varities of trees and shrubs. The 18th century house, which was gutted by fire in 1974 has an innovative new use, incorporating a terrace restaurant overlooking the garden and speciality shops.

Enniskerry, Co. Wicklow
t: +44 1 204 6000
www.powerscourt.ie

Trengwainton Garden:

Trengwainton, which in Cornish means 'house of spring', is a plantsman's paradise. The favourable climate allows many rare plants to be grown unprotected against frost. The unusual walled garden, constructed in 1820 for early vegetable crops, now houses a wonderful collection of trees and shrubs. Some rhododendrons flowered at Trengwainton for the first time in the UK after being collected by the renowned plant hunter Frank Kingdon-Ward. As well as its stunning collections of rhododendrons, camellias and magnolias, the garden has a stream running almost its entire length, with plantings of astilbe, primula and New Zealand tree ferns.

A walk to the top of the garden gives magnificent views over Mount's Bay.

Trengwainton Garden, Madron, Penzance, Cornwall, TR20 8RZ
t: +44 1736 363148
trengwainton@nationaltrust.org.uk
www.nationaltrust.org.uk

Arboretum:

Frank & Rachel Doyle founded Arboretum Garden Centre in 1978. From humble beginnings, they have grown to be one of the best garden centres in Ireland. What does arboretum mean? Arboretum is Latin for a 'collection of trees'. The Arboretum Garden Centre is a state of the art gardening and lifestyle experience, aiming to bring you a totally customer focused shopping experience. At the Arboretum they pride themselves on attention to detail. Highly trained staff are on hand to help you with all your needs from gardening advice to choosing the perfect gift! Indeed it is their high level of customer service, the range of products and friendly welcome that has earned the title of "Bord Bia – Best customer service 2006/2007 Bord Bia Garden Centre of the Year and Irelands first five star garden centre.

Kilkenny Road, Leighlinbridge, Co Carlow, Ireland.
t: +353 59 9721558
www.arboretum.ie

Bloom 2008:

Ireland's largest annual gardening event takes places from 29th May to 2nd June 2008 Thousands of flowers and plants, extraordinary gardens, Seminars and shopping.... One Unmissable Event!
Bloom 2008, Ireland's largest gardening showcase is set to return from Thursday 29th May to Monday 2nd June inclusive. Bloom is organised by Bord Bia, the Irish Food Board, with responsibility for the promotion and development of Ireland's horticulture industry. The event takes place in the heart of Dublin in the Phoenix Park and is set to tantalise visitors with an array of new and exciting features to view, sense and savour. For further information visit www.bloominthepark.com

Get on line today and make the most important date in your diary for 2008.

Bloom, celebrate garden life

Formality:

Formality is established as Ireland's leading garden boutique retailer with extensive ranges of garden related merchandise. As a premier supplier of garden furniture, Formality exclusively sells Tribu furniture from Belgium, in conjunction with other ranges from France and Britain. Summer 2008 sees the introduction of some furniture from Belgium, offering a contemporary take on traditional, all weather rattan furniture. Formality is a principal provider of topiary and architectural specimen plants, with an extensive range of planters in copper, lead, teak, terrazzo and zinc. Formality's seasonal decorative ranges offer both contemporary and traditional collections, with a unifying theme of clean crisp lines. We carry a wide range of accessories for both indoor and outdoor use and 'must-have' items for the visionary gardener. Formality also offers a comprehensive garden design service.
Formality at the Cowshed, Glasthule, Co. Dublin.
t:+ 353 1 280 8071 info@formalityonline.com
www.formalityonline.com

Johnstown Garden Centre:

Johnstown Garden Centre, Naas, at junction 8 on the main N7 route from Dublin to the South is one of the longest established garden centres in the country. Founded in 1974 by John and Elsie Clarke, the company has evolved to be one of the premier plant centres in Europe. The centre is very proud to offer the entire range exclusively to Irish Gardeners from Hillier's, Blooms of Bressingham, and Notcutts Nurseries from England, together with the very best premium quality plants from Irish and European growers.
Johnstown offers easy access, extensive parking, and a Café . A very large indoor shop stocks the very latest in Garden Care, Home Furnishings and décor that is very different from the usual high street shops.
Well worth a visit with something for all the family.

t: +353 45 879138
www.johnstowngardencentre.ie

Mount Venus Nursery:

Specialising in hardy perennials, border plants, ornamental grasses, woodland plants, bamboo, and a good range of unusual trees, shrubs and climbers, Mount Venus has gained a reputation for providing variety and professional advice becoming a favourite for garden designers and enthusiasts throughout Ireland.
Liat and Oliver Schurmann have gained international recognition for their exquisite design work winning many prestigious awards (e.g.: Hampton Court Palace Flower Show . 2005 Silver-gilt for 'Walk On Water' and 2007 Silver -gilt for their unforgettable 'Infinity Garden'). Their broad knowledge of plants and their accessibility as a nursery enables them to create detailed and diverse planting schemes, achieving a well balanced plant society resulting in sustainability and low maintenance, always with the ecological approach in mind.

The Walled Garden Tibradden
Mutton Lane,Rathfarnham, Dublin 16
t:+353 14933813, +353 863218789,
schurmann@ireland.com, www.mountvenusnursery.com
Open times Mon- Sat 10am-6pm Closed Jan-Feb

Powerscourt Garden Pavilion:

State of the art barbeques, garden furniture and saunas are just three of the surprises at Powerscourt Garden Pavilion in Enniskerry, Co Wicklow. Outstanding is the 4 Seasons range of furniture, exclusive to Bridgman, which is equally suitable for the garden, the deck or the conservatory....and the assembly and delivery service removes the stress of your purchase. Add 25,000 sq ft of house and conservatory plants, patio plants, and shrubs of the highest quality, great garden gadgetry, delicate porcelain bowls, exquisite wicker furniture and a huge range of gifts and the added value of Powerscourt Garden Pavilion becomes obvious. The drive up the legendary Powerscourt beech avenue is enough by itself to make a visit to Powerscourt Garden Pavilion worthwhile. Add ample parking, just a few yards from the stunning glass structure and it is clear why Powerscourt Garden Pavilion is such an outstanding shopping experience.

t: +353 1 204 6014

Scalp Wood Nurseries:

Scalp Wood Nurseries nestles in the foothills of the Dublin Mountains, on the Enniskerry Road, opposite the Hotel and Ski Slope. From humble beginnings in 1975, Scalp Wood Nurseries have grown to become one of Ireland's leading suppliers of hardy Exterior European specimen plants, bamboos, trees shrubs and topiary. Our selective range of plants and trees are individually selected to provide customers with an extensive range of quality stock. Our years of experience enable us to provide excellent customer service from friendly and enthusiastic staff. At Scalp Wood Nurseries our philosophy is simple: through our partnership with you, we will transform your home into a living, growing legacy of natural beauty.
Our Garden "A TUSCAN PARADISE" at Bloom 2007 showcased the diverse range of plants we now offer (from Lavanders to Mature Olive Trees). To create your own Irish Paradise come and visit us.

Scalp Wood Nurseries, Enniskerry Road, Kilternan,
Dublin 18, t: +353 1 295 4636
www.scalpwood.com

Tadpole:

A truly unique, bespoke manufacturing company specialising in "one off" design and production of unusual objects. Founder, Stuart Sharpless, has created bespoke items for private and corporate clients, designers and architects around the globe for over 15 years. We've become experts in our field and recently featured in the RTE series "I want a garden" with Diarmuid Gavin, in which we project managed and built the centre piece for two gardens. We pride ourselves on the variety and quality of work we have produced, reflected in our impressive client list which includes architects Foster & Partners and Richard Rogers, designers Andrew Martin and Villiers Brothers, Corporate Banks and prestigious Hotels. Commissions from pieces of furniture, to sculptures, outdoor rooms, kitchens and water features as well as roof gardens, bespoke lighting and staircases. With our knowledge and expertise we can realise your ideas regardless of how ambitious they may seem.

info@tadpole.ie www.tadpole.ie

garden rooms, glasshouses & furniture

Bellissima:

Bellissima believe that outdoor spaces are as important a style statement as indoor spaces. Choose a space under open sky and view it as an extension of your home, then furnish it with beautiful things. In our outdoor courtyard you can view the internationally renowned Gloster range. Gloster have been making furniture for over 40 years and customers can choose from teak, sling or woven furniture in a variety of styles from classic to contemporary. Gloster understand that outdoor furniture needs to exist in a tougher environment than indoor furniture and invests heavily in the technology necessary to create weather resistant materials, designed to last. The materials used in certain ranges are suitable for coastal areas and are maintenance free.

Bellissima's interior designers continue to provide the now renowned level of customer service and a large range of unique outdoor accessories are available to create a truly individual alfresco look.

Bellissima, Bypass Road, Bandon, Co. Cork.
t: +353 23 54740 www.bellissima.ie

Dedon:

DEDON is the world renowned leading brand for the widest collection of woven style outdoor furniture. The talents of some of the most diverse people from around the globe are entwined in DEDON's furniture. Skilled craftsmen from Asia, fibre developers from Europe, and designers from many different countries create timeless works of art that are suitable for everyday use. At Maison & Objet in Paris, DEDON presented three new collections Zofa, Phoenix and Spa to compliment the stunning ranges Orbit, Hemisphere and Obelisk. The From traditional dining sets, exotic sunloungers –Leaf - to the absolutely stunning signature pieces such as Orbit-Yin/Yang-Obelisk-Daydream, the collections cover every conceivable desire for outdoor relaxation.

Each piece is individually hand woven, using the original DEDON fibre. The collection is weather resistant, UV stabilised and designed to withstand the extremes of sun, snow and saltwater.

Each collection offers the ability to create an inspiring and appealing living style. www.leisureplan.co.uk

Ego:

The Ego ethos is design excellence and exclusivity with a hint of audacity. Suggesting excellence and creating desire through their pure form and noble materials, each piece will seduce you offering you long-lasting enjoyment. In the words of Ego's creator Thomas Sauvage; "A promise of relaxation and a moment of egoism , your egoism - and mine too- for spending a privileged moment in time to materialize my desires by sculpting fluid lines just for you. Collection Premiere is the creation of custom-built furniture, built to your own tastes by associating different colours and a choice of materials.

Collection Premiere is the creation of custom-built furniture, personally built to your own tastes by associating different colours and a choice of materials.

Tandem Collection is the inspiration of it's creator Thomas Sauvage: conviviality, function and modularity.

Kama Collection is an innovative, amusing modular approach to outdoor living. Just by re-positioning the one-size cushion can change the whole seating arrangements. www.leisureplan.co.uk

Fischer-Mobel:

Established since 1984, the Fischer-Mobel brand represents well designed high quality outdoor furniture. Fischer-Mobel means innovation over monotony, quality over mass production, functionality over simply useful. Multiple international design awards confirm the recognition their products have enjoyed from independent organisations. for a knowledge and passion for contemporary design. Using the very latest high-tech materials, the Fischer-Mobel collections are selected for the customer who requires a minimalist look without compromising quality. Emphasis on materials with durability gives the collections exceptional weathering qualities. From frames with either high grade stainless steel or hard powder coated aluminium, matched with dimensionally stable, tear proof slings (collections Air and Swing) to fm-foam, a new light fast and weatherproof seating material, extensively used and tested in the automotive industry. (Kyoto) with table tops in fm-ceramtop, a scratch and frost proof ceramic material, completes a collections which offers the ultimate in maintenance free outdoor living. www.leisureplan.co.uk

Hampton Conservatories:

Hampton Conservatories is one of the leading hardwood conservatory manufacturers in the UK and Ireland. Established for 25 Years, a large variety of clients have been catered for, including private home owners, property developers, hotel groups, and numerous architectural practises. We offer complete project management from conception and design through to completion. With environmental considerations to the fore, all timber used in a Hampton conservatory is sourced from managed forestation programmes.

Four main products are offered:

• Bespoke conservatories and Orangeries: Thoughtfully designed for their environment, they are like no other room in the house.

• Commercial Conservatories: This method of using commercial space can be practical and cost effective.

• Botanical Architecture: Specialising in the replacement of 17th to 19th century original glasshouses.

• Pool houses: Creating an environment that gives year-round use of the pool.

www.hamptonconservatories.co.uk
t: +44 (0) 870 240 6093

Marston & Langinger:

Founded in 1978, Marston & Langinger is the market leader in bespoke glass buildings including garden rooms, conservatories, orangeries, poolhouses and greenhouses. M & L have designed and built prestigious projects worldwide. As well as showrooms in London and New York, the company has a studio in Dublin where senior designer, Sharon O'Callaghan, offers a personal design service throughout Ireland. Each M & L glass building is designed from scratch and built to an exceptional standard of design and craftsmanship using sustainable materials and up-to-the minute technology. The end result is a unique building that fits perfectly with the house and its setting, helping to bring the scents, colours and textures of the garden inside. An interior designer works on each project, ensuring that the lighting, flooring and furnishings make the new room become a stylish and welcoming part of the home.

Ireland: 1 800 635 081
London: 192 Ebury Street, London, SW1W 8UP
t: +44 (0) 207 881 5700
www.marston-and-langinger.ie

Quest:

Quest Interiors is located just 3 minutes from Dublin's Christchurch Cathedral on Francis Street, where proprietor Kieran Morrin, a member of the Irish antique dealers association, has been trading for over 22 years. Specialists in French antique pieces for both interiors and exteriors, Quest interiors carry a stunning and unique collection of garden furniture including a beautiful range of exquisite French wirework balcony furniture and arches and Roman antique stone effect tables and benches. The Quest collection also includes charming Georgian and Victorian traditional terracotta pieces, cast iron garden seats and both traditional and contemporary water fountains, features, statuary and much, much more.

For further information and to view the whole collection call into Quest Interiors, 37 Francis Street, Dublin8
t: +353 1 4540299

Shomera:

At Shomera we design creative living space for contemporary life. By using the highest quality craftsmanship and natural materials we create unique rooms of the very best design, comfort and style.

We could all enhance our lifestyles with an additional room for relaxing, entertaining or even working from home. For almost a decade we have helped people improve their lifestyle by adding additional living space to their property. You can be confident that your investment in a Shomera will improve the value of your property as well as your standard of living.

With the guidance of our design team, you can choose to create a stand alone Shomera Studio or a Shomera Extension incorporated onto the house. Whichever style you choose, your Shomera will be custom made for you and designed to blend in with the aesthetics of your property and its environment.

t: +353 1 825 8288
info@shomera.ie www.shomera.ie

Elma Fenton:

Elma Fenton, ecological landscape architect, also trades as Ellen Landscape Designs providing an innovative and sensitive approach to transforming exterior spaces through pure design. Combining practicality with creative flair, producing spaces that surprise and enchant. Imaginative and realistic solutions are developed in close liaison with client needs. Attention to details such as structures, textures and materials help to unify the design. Elma Fenton has worked on a wide spectrum of projects both in Ireland and abroad, including exhibiting award winning main show gardens at Chelsea Flower Show 2005 & Bloom 2007 which both feature an ecological swimming ponds. Further projects have included residential design and build commissions, commercial projects, schools, parks and detailed planting plans, specifications and showcase gardens. Elma is a landscape architect, garden designer and horticulturalist.
Elma Fenton, 7 Cowper Road, Dublin 6,
t/f: +353 1 497 7311, m: +353 86 812 2396
Garden Studio, Monasterevin Co. Kildare
www.ellenlandscapedesigns.com, www.elmafenton.ie

Garden and Landscape Designers Association:

The GLDA was established over ten years ago to set and maintain the highest professional standards in garden and landscape design. Each designer has an in-depth understanding of all aspects of the design process from site evaluation, through concept design, to the selection of structures, plants and materials best suited to your taste and style. All members are rigorously evaluated by a panel of external examiners in order to gain full membership status. The GLDA organise regular professional development workshops, seminars and garden tours, as well as producing the quarterly publication Compass. For a full list of members and to find a designer to meet your requirements, log onto our website:

t: +353 1 294 0092.
info@glda.ie
www.glda.ie

Howbert and Mays:

Howbert and Mays, the garden design partnership of Anthea Howbert and Tycho Mays is the creative force behind many of Ireland's most beautiful gardens. From the smallest city garden to the most expansive country estate, Howbert and Mays create gardens which are both classic and contemporary. With years of experience and training, their trademarks are lively and dynamic planting schemes, high-quality materials, and designs which relate intelligently to their environment. They take the garden-making process from conception to completion, and are frequently asked to stay on to guide the garden through its ongoing development. Howbert and Mays have an established working relationship with many of Ireland's best architects and are often consulted right from the beginning of the architectural process. Howbert and Mays create enduring designs which transcend trend and are designed to last.

t: +353 404 49819
tycho@eircom.net www.howbertandmays.ie

Paula Ryan:

A graduate of the renowned Inchbald School of garden design, Paula Ryan's work has featured in books and magazines in the UK and has been showcased in the Garden Makers series with Joe Swift. Paula has exhibited at Chelsea Flower Show, most recently being awarded a Silver medal for her Amnesty International Garden of Human Rights in 2007. With many years experience of both commercial and private projects Paula Ryan prides herself on interpreting her clients' needs to sympathetically develop the garden of their dreams. With careful use of materials Paula works to integrate the garden with the house and the local area. Combining naturalistic planting with clean lines and simple geometry she maximises space, interest and light in gardens small and large. Often collaborating with other design professionals such as Architects and interior designers Paula brings a thoroughly professional approach to garden design.
t: +44 208123 8935 / +353 1 289 3575
www.paularyangardens.com

Setanta Landscapes:

Setanta Landscapes is Dublin's leading provider of one-stop garden services. Our services include: Gardening - Garden maintenance/Clean-up's, plants & planting, fencing and new lawns laid. Our team includes qualified horticulturists, who can advise on lawns and lawn care, plants and planting plans. Our garden maintenance team can provide a seasonal clean-up for your garden or regular monthly/weekly/bi-weekly garden maintenance services. Our Tree Surgery Services include tree removal, crown thinning/lifting reduction, hedge trim and stump grinding. Our Tree Surgery team are all highly qualified and experienced Tree Surgeons. Our objective is to improve the appearance and promote the healthy growth of your trees.
We at Setanta are committed to the wider environment, which is why we aim to have 100% of all green waste we remove recycled in accordance with the best international industry standards.

14 Eastmoreland Place, Ballsbridge, Dublin 4
t: +353 1 667 5861
enquiries@setantalandscapes.com

Sinéad Finn Landscapes:

Sinéad Finn Landscapes offers a comprehensive, and award winning, landscape and garden design service. We work with our clients to create exactly the type of design they want. We believe that the success of any garden design solution lies in meeting clients' needs, tastes and lifestyles in a realistic yet creative way, with the greatest attention to detail. To this end, we work closely with clients to ensure the finished design will both delight and excite the senses, while also being accessible and usable. Clients are presented with a complete booklet containing the garden master plan, associated planting plans and advice on plant maintenance.
Sinéad Finn Landscapes: Awarded Silver Medal in the Small Garden Category for 'Haven', Bloom 2007.

t: +353 87 989 0910
mail@sineadfinn.com www.sineadfinn.com

Thirtythreetrees:

Based in Dublin, Thirtythreetrees is a design led Landscape Architecture/ Garden Design practice established by Co-Directors Jimi Shields and Maria Vlahos in 2004. Jimi, also a senior tutor at UCD School of Architecture, is a trained architect while Maria, (previously Head Gardener at the prestigious Mount Usher Gardens) is a professional Horticulturist.
The company has collaborated with many renowned architects including de Paor Architects, Grafton Architects, Mc Garry NiEanaigh, Derek Tynan Architects and Douglas Wallace Architects. Projects awarded to the practice to date range in scale from bespoke urban gardens, public open space and healthcare to hotel and leisure. Following on from their work at the g Hotel, Thirtythreetrees have again been appointed by Monogram Hotels to design a garden for The Magistrates Court Hotel in Covent Garden, London.
Thirtythreetrees are currently working on a variety of projects from conceptual design to construction.

t: +353 1 496 6813 info@thirtythreetrees.com,
www.thirtythreetrees.com

Virgoe McEnery:

We want to grow your green space into something spectacular! Let us show you how!
We are a landscaping company that specializes in delivering something unique for every client. We provide a professional assessment of your existing green space, and offer a choice of options that will bring both value and beauty to your landscape. We design & build, project manage, and maintain. We bring to completion any landscaping project: domestic, commercial or public. We are members of the ALCI, are fully insured and have built an impressive profile of both hard and soft landscaping projects. Our staff are professionally experienced, trained and certified in all aspects of landscaping. They are backed up by our qualified management team who monitor the progress of each project to a satisfactory completion. Give us a call and we will work with you to see nature at her best in your green space!

Virgoe McEnery Landscaping Ltd.
Fairways, Balheary, Swords, Co Dublin.
t: +353 1 840 7674, m: +353 86 170 8146
info@vmce.ie, www.vmce.ie

credits

Gardens in an urban landscape:

wall to wall
Photography by Helen Fickling
www.helenfickling.com
www.chdesigns.co.uk

moonstruck
Photography by Helen Fickling
www.helenfickling.com
www.andysturgeon.com

a seamless blend
Photography by Helen Fickling
www.helenfickling.com
www.whcgardendesign.com

a city haven
Photography by Barry Murphy
www.barrymurphyphotography.com
www.the-hempel.co.uk
www.anouskahempeldesign.com

watson's world
Photography by Helen Fickling
www.helenfickling.com
www.patrickwatson.co.za

structure and harmony
Photography by Helen Fickling
www.helenfickling.com
www.christopherbradley-hole.co.uk
www.ericparryarchitects.co.uk

coastal sanctuary
Photography by Studio 77
www.studioseventyseven.com
Philip Brightling Landscapes: +353 (0) 12877179
Murphy & Wood Garden Centre: +353 (0) 12854855

Gardens on Show:

historical elegance
Photography by Studio 77
www.studioseventyseven.com
www.robertmyers-associates.co.uk
www.fortnumandmason.com
www.rhs.org.uk/chelsea

an english garden
Photography by Studio 77
www.studioseventyseven.com
www.chrisbeardshaw.com
www.nationaltrust.org.uk/hidcote
www.rhs.org.uk/chelsea

natural habitat
Photography by Studio 77
www.studioseventyseven.com
www.fetzer.com
katefrey@mac.com
www.rhs.org.uk/chelsea

a plantsman's garden
Photography by Studio 77
www.studioseventyseven.com
www.land-art.co.uk
www.telegraph.co.uk
www.rhs.org.uk/chelsea

journey of life
Photography by Studio 77
www.studioseventyseven.com
www.jinnyblom.com
www.laurent-perrier.com
www.rhs.org.uk/chelsea

a swedish legacy
Photography by Studio 77
www.studioseventyseven.com
www.linneaus2007.se
ulf.nordnordfjell@ramboll.se
www.rhs.org.uk/chelsea

bold reflections
Photography by Studio 77
www.studioseventyseven.com
www.trevortooth.com
www.lloydstsb.com
www.rhs.org.uk/chelsea

on golden pond
Photography by Studio 77
www.studioseventyseven.com
www.diarmuidgavindesigns.co.uk
www.gardenhealth.com
www.rhs.org.uk/chelsea

natural exuberance
Photography by Studio 77
www.studioseventyseven.com
www.andysturgeon.com
www.cancerresearch.org.uk
www.rhs.org.uk/chelsea

rooftop escape
Photography by Studio 77
www.studioseventyseven.com
www.paularyangardens.com
www.rhs.org.uk/chelsea

garden of the sun
Photography by Studio 77
www.studioseventyseven.com
www.cycas.com.au
www.flemings.com.au/chelsea2007
www.rhs.org.uk/chelsea

mission to mars
Photography by Studio 77
www.studioseventyseven.com
www.600dayswithbradstone.com
www.rhs.org.uk/chelsea

striking form
Photography by Helen Fickling
www.helenfickling.com
www.tadpole.ie
www.rhs.org.uk/chelsea

fountain of life
Photography by Studio 77
www.studioseventyseven.com
www.janemccorkelllandscape.ie
www.keelings.com
www.bloominthepark.com

natural connection
Photography by Studio 77
www.studioseventyseven.com
www.elmafenton.ie
www.bloominthepark.com

perfect proportions
Photography by Studio 77
www.studioseventyseven.com
www.paulmartindesigns.com
www.bloominthepark.com

blossoming bright
Photography by Studio 77
www.studioseventyseven.com
www.rhs.org.uk/chelsea

Gardens with a story to tell:

emerald treasure
Photography by Studio 77
www.studioseventyseven.com
& Des Irwin- Pages: 76-91
www.mountushergardens.com
www.avoca.ie

the rose garden
Photography by Helen Fickling
www.helenfickling.com
www.kifsgate.co.uk

true to nature
Photography by Helen Fickling
www.helenfickling.com
www.gravetyemanor.co.uk

great expectations
Photography by Studio 77
www.studioseventyseven.com
www.corkelodge.com

What's on your coffee table?

Subscribe to Ireland's most exclusive
Design Book Collection

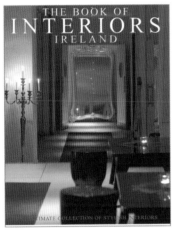

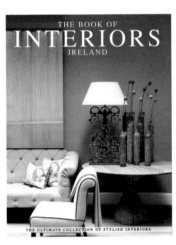

To subscribe, simply log onto www.montaguegroup.ie

email subscriptions@montaguegroup.ie or tel: +353 (0)1 669 2101